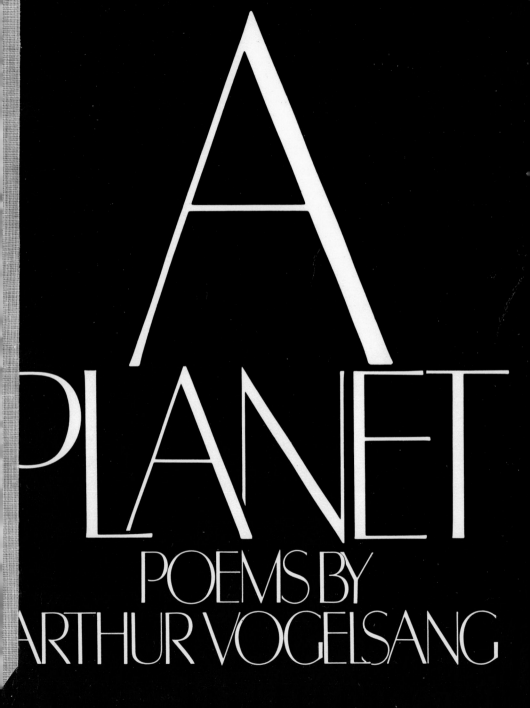

A PLANET

POEMS BY
ARTHUR VOGELSANG

A PLANET

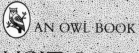 AN OWL BOOK

HOLT, RINEHART AND WINSTON
NEW YORK

A PLANET

POEMS BY
ARTHUR VOGELSANG

Copyright © 1983 by Arthur Vogelsang
Published by Holt, Rinehart and Winston, 383 Madison Avenue,
New York, New York 10017.
Published simultaneously in Canada by Holt, Rinehart and Winston of Canada,
Limited.

Library of Congress Cataloging in Publication Data
Vogelsang, Arthur.
A planet.
I. Title.
PS3572.O297P5 1982   813'.54   82-9273
ISBN: 0-03-062107-0   AACR2

First Edition
Designer: Elissa Ichiyasu
Printed in the United States of America
10   9   8   7   6   5   4   3   2   1

ISBN 0-03-062107-0

Acknowledgment is made to the following magazines for poems
which first appeared in them:

Antaeus, "Circles and Waves," "Poem (Here on Mars . . .)"; *The Ark River Review,*
"Acting Simple," "Come Here," "Sitting at Home," "Swollen Sonnet"; *Ascent,*
"Correspondents"; *The Back Door,* "Yoking"; *Carolina Quarterly,* "Poem (It's the famous
sun. . . .)," "The Radio, The Norton Anthology"; *The Chowder Review,* "The
Companion"; *Epoch,* "The Clouds"; *The Iowa Review,* "Christmas, 1968; Sister, 13,"
"Correspondences," "Drive Imagining," "Letter to Shakespeare," "The Picture," "What to
Say"; *Kansas Quarterly,* "A Package of Magazines," "A Tour of 'Civilisation' at the Wichita
Art Museum," "Dolly Out," "Editing at Home with a Sick Woman," "Feeling That Way
Too"; *The Little Magazine,* "Here, There"; *The Midwest Quarterly,* "The Singer"; *Northwest
Review,* "Deer Herd Brings Puma to Kansas"; *Panache,* "Tornado Reading in the
Morning"; *The Paris Review,* "Indian Summer in North America," "Poem (Sometimes if
you've been in and out . . .)"; *Partisan Review,* "August, N. Linn St.," "California," "The
Vein"; *Ploughshares,* "A Little Crazy," "My Shoes," "The Night"; *Poetry Northwest,*
"Another Fake Love Poem"; *The Seattle Review,* "Presently"; *Shenandoah,* "Domestic Poem
in Egypt"; *Three Rivers Poetry Journal,* "Proletariat," "Saturday."

"Deer Herd Brings Puma to Kansas" also appeared in *Best Poems of 1973*, the Borestone
Mountain Poetry Awards.

Thanks to the National Endowment for the Arts for a grant during the writing
of some of these poems.

CONTENTS

ONE

A COUNTRY

DRIVE IMAGINING

I'm speeding west somewhere in the top of Ohio or Indiana,
And to my right is the Arctic Circle, all white and scary.
It is very dark and cold
But my car is very powerful, shut, and too warm.
To my left is super-powerful New Orleans Radio 87,
Beaming girl singers with crooked jaws.
I test you by asking the time but
You trust me to not give you the wheel while you're sleeping.
Your mouth is like the curve of the earth for fifty miles on flat ice.
Out loud, unevenly, I say where the road right goes. No answer.

Your skirt is high and little,
Filling the front of the car with pounds of white.
My nails raise the flesh there;
Electricity from the big dots and standing hair sends the radio signal
Into a trough. Eyes shut, you are awake
Enough to say, I can't breathe, fix the heat.
You sigh and lean back like a snowflake pressing into a marshmallow.
The urge to ask your advice about the possible right turn
To Battle Creek, Canada, and you-know-where
Is a malignant lump in my chest, like facing the dark makes.

And at what point would we drive out onto the nothing but ice?
Cresting she says, Hello truck drivers,
And mentions a more powerful flashlight for them to buy.
That's the trouble with global capabilities,
You can be fighting icebergs and some joker will yodel
In your ear, "You are my sunshine . . ."

I shout that the road right goes you-know-where.
Eyes shut, you are awake enough to say,
All that's stopping us is a lack of gas stations,
My twisted mouth around your fear.

CALIFORNIA

Everyone has some trees, and I wanted to take you out under mine,
The hairy shady ones and the ones with firecrackers hanging down naturally
Or fastened by me, I wanted to abandon this phony voice
As we went through the patio or if it screamed don't leave me Jesus I'll die
As we passed through the nice garden dragging it clamped tooth and
       nail to our cuffs
And it had a headache from the even, massive hedges,
From the sight of women in grief and sexy
In nightgowns in the increasing light through doorways,
I would keep the house for it, little fierce violent doll with big teeth
Jerking around the house biting the furniture,
And live out under these trees speaking directly like a saint
And simply like a good man, altering by degrees the gas flame of my
       portable power,
To you and to those youngsters beyond the fence off a ways,
Cheering, at a distance, and the 4 billion beyond them.

Everyone who had a life in the evil ugly desert knew he would get lucky
Some day, either a huge herd of fat lambs would rampage
Over the dunes, dune after dune, shitting to a depth of 6 inches,
Rich shit spreading like an insane river,
Or it would rain *there*, and not there, and the Russians would die and *he*
       would live.
Most in these tribes had unnatural, half-baked voices like mine
In prayer but like you did not believe in apocalypse
As from bombs or a sour mist mixing volatilely with sand
As I believed, for they lived near an unfilled river
Whose substance filled their souls and grew a city of fat, wet fruit.

By the way, there is a soul, and not just people
To love—Jews, Arabs, sand, oil, and poetry,
The holy geography of little hills and great trains the odor of solder—
Or perhaps there is not.

Days went by when driving itself was a pleasure and when it wasn't I would
Turn around for an instant—on a white silver screen
Men who can build tires from wood and turn nuts and dance, who have
        seductive
Many toned voices thrown in the service of their lord, country, or ranch
        foreman
Are traveling great distances to fight beasts
Like redskins or the brute Hector for the love of a red-haired girl.
Or when one mile was too far I had a reverie on a crest, houses
        contemporary, glass—
I saw our roof way down there, below it the bed of a dry river
        primordial, further
Down on the royal road Spanish sliced heads till the hair peeled loose.
The sun was pure enjoyment. Second gear,
Dropping in the little blunt hills of the massacre,
A cloud slowly pivots to the shape of a hook,
Like iron and oil so deliberately turning to that one house
Upon the leaping, spiralling planet.

ANOTHER FAKE LOVE POEM

Years later you are the way you should be, making tidal waves
At meetings, surviving the concussions of your own poems,
And making hundreds of dollars a month.
And suddenly you remember it was *your* fault.
And it wasn't just a crack in the personality crust,
It was the strong, definite beginning of the way you've become.

There must be a planet where the people get sad and die
When there are no earthquakes,
And when one is coming they are happy and
Go to Italian restaurants all over the planet in their Italy,
Their England, their Baltimore, and laugh happily and
Drink wine and make sweet dirty talk
As magnitudinous tremors pass through their wicker chairs.

She's in Canada now, and once went to China,
And when you go to Chile to accept the personality-
In-literature prize and to Antarctica to make a speech,
There it will be, *your* fault, waving, roaring, or hurrying near,
Way behind, harmless and ugly.
The thought of yourself as an ass makes you happy
But you will get sad and die.

WHAT TO SAY

TO M.S.

The train's speed, the gray and blurry Atlantic Plateau
A bitter sight, and a few stray gin wings buzzing "left behind"
Most of the time, and in that trip past water,
Past swamps, and over water, I must have ridden by some dead women
Submerged and totally rejected as in murder
By fancy, brutal, heavy-drinking beaus.

Nothing's worse. Though there's your loneliness on brilliant days at 2
That even the hardest fucker who loves you truly for months
Can't poke away. Sometimes it's like sinking too fast from floor to floor.

Or that disgust if you can't think of the most important thing
Or say it. When I was in the train the train dominated the landscape
And I thought and thought. I'd be at my desk (this is a story) and

That story, my medium-sized angular cactus sitting in clay,
It and the window at arm's length, like
The thunder, and coffee like a musty repellant against a buzzing nothing,
That story of the window in front of me
Has no middle, like a cube of ice only a half hour old,
As if the rain that begins to bang away at the ground
Were the center of what I swore to say.

Then there's a speed worse than sex or elevators,
When each year goes by like Arlington or Perryville,
Actual like houses or the actual words death and loneliness.

DOMESTIC POEM IN EGYPT

My hand is making funny signs in your
Lap and we are panting and gasping at each of your
Jokes as if you were some new dirty
Phrase driving us to hysteria. A book is on there too and
Sand in the binding is deep and grinds and grates
At the turn of a page, like typing from within a tomb.
On a famous view of Egypt reproduced, a scratch.
As if a tiny stone cat sat on your lap?
Nor are we in that photograph, but we were once. Do
You remember coming upon the big pointy tomb
Of pharaoh Rameses? We were chilled to the
Nipples at the freezing air hurrying up into our faces.
There was a rubber walkway all the way into the depths
Of the tomb, an example of irony you said
You know like a rubber vein through Rameses' spirit.
A little further on on the next page
Is this picture of Emma Jung and her husband and 46 friends
All practically grinning at a meeting in 1911.
Perhaps someone has said watch the birdie in
The middle of a huge silence. She is
Small, dark, and sexy. They are
Amused either at being photographed
Or at the inkblot on the next page
Which is seared open in the middle and bulges at each side.

INDIAN SUMMER IN NORTH AMERICA

The last warm night,
Sleep after ugly crying,
And we're under a sheet staring up
Like drifting on our backs in Florida
Lonely or small in the ocean as we are so
I was black drunk last night
And walking to work (it gets hotter all day)
Among many leaves I step on a letter
That begins I love you dearly.
I bend and the booze, a splinter, slides into place;
I stand and it shifts like fog crossing a summer
River. As I read (the lovers are nameless) my friends are sliding
Into revolving chairs in nine parts of the country, ghosts
That crouch like dancers at a distance in the woods.
The letter uses no names, first or last. It says
I love you dearly. And
I'm sorry. Sorry, sorry, sorry. Then
It gets stupid and proposes a deal.
A plane is circling and floating into place,
An old girl friend (she's palpable, standing close)
Is fishing on a wide river
Buoyed by today's rough warm water.
Everyone dear in all those states will go home
And have a beer or a whiskey
But it's afternoon and your voice on the phone
Is sliding on the back of my head
And, get ready, we look up together—
Those are people drifting down like leaves
Toward you and I think toward me.

SATURDAY

The mailman like the sun lifts luck out of his sack
lifting his arms kindly and it's morning
like a new lung in a sore, raw chest.

You are as authentic as water
and are beside a strange plant whose name I can't
remember, a corn plant I think, whatever

That is, but your name and your arms
are very clear to me as the light that keeps coming
through the window surrounds them totally like planned light in a film.

Like the persistent white liars whose many baskets of terrible joy
daily surround my chair in other rooms
I keep at and keep at a particular lucidity,

That is, I am staring at your arms and the light,
but this is like a foolish string lace container ripping
with the several pounds of my heart.

Finally rain at dusk tosses up the smell of the grass
and you hold tight, whispering "bad luck, bad luck."

AMERICANS IN AN ORANGE GROVE

"I became insane with long intervals of horrible sanity."
—Poe

No such luck under the lush, bumpy orange and leaf sky, the owner
A Cuban uncle of your wife's friend, his humble precise English,
The efficient, expansive Land-Rover, three mild, smart women past
Nubility, white folds of their lips, and I swear seemingly pure
Asses hanging out a little in shorts in the healthy, musty grove. Excuse
Me. Far from your home base of drinking and consistent madness you
The man, the poet, muse upon the wonder of civ, the grafting
Of lemons and oranges on the same twig ilization
The long arm of the American police, benign pluck
Of a kind, productive, intelligent uncle from the spite of the Communists.
No such luck, you weak bastard, you'll have to bathe in the bath-
Like hot sea and eat the lamb (we're
Having later tonight) with sensible, luxuriant women and get tired, sleep
No prowling corridors alone for promiscuous screams. Sleep. A short nasty
Wind overhead, fierce for sure & w. teeth & a storm
Of oranges before which all run but you, the poet, the man, behold
Yourself, victim of a juicy bombardment, ridiculous loony survivor. Twinges
Of desire in the loins of the enchanted women. In this split-
Second all others but you are utterly happy tho they stare and think
"It won't be all right in the end, it just won't."

COME HERE

"He knew how to say many false things that were like true sayings."
—ODYSSEY

Dear, snow to the windowsill today has kept me
Playing my tape recording of our endless talk yesterday. In it
There is a grin on my face and a phone in my face
And outside is air from some great orbital refrigerator open on my house;
It may be this space box of wind and machines took that picture on TV
Of the storm our country is superimposed on
And barely adequate to in size, blowing east,
Which will be here when the sun goes down at your end of the phone
Shortly in three hours when it will look like Antarctica here ha
Ha But we have *sunny* you say three times *sunny sunny* days
Here you lonesome lonesome boy.

I say I'll tell you a story in a whisper over our cloudy connection,
Take your pants off. Listeners around the fire
Get closer to your loved one and take your pants off. I
Have a housekeeper who gives me a shower
Each day, she's crazy about me and would play with my thick scar
If I had one or my beard if I had one of those.
Now deep into the dirty story—do you like it? you begin to cry or cough
Or this noise is those listeners who haven't been there
For 2900 years, though they were once, this noise
Is some of those listeners getting hot and coming so many centuries ago
From the story which I have not told completely though it is on the recording
Or this is you.
                    On the phone is a little rubber cup

And a wire from that cup to my recorder; each reel is turning easily
Like the earth and if you could see how gently the machine is moving,
The wire swaying surely in its determination to remember each word,
You'd get such a grip
On yourself you could tell stories for ten years and you start to. No,
I hadn't heard that an actor dressed as a warrior scattered people in panic
And killed a few slowly and painfully with a big knife out your way.
It is possible in an eastern city to have adventures
Of a military kind if you want to be a mass murderer
And give up your own life but I can't say I've done that
Mostly because in this city of lawyers all I have to do
To look ridiculous is stand in the outer doorway or gate to my garden
Wearing a helmet and carrying shield and two spears
Or walk up and down Walnut Street that way. So they'll never know
From my spears that death is soon and marriage is painful.
Meanwhile our voices are urgent and thrilling enough to fool the goddess
Who came down today in miraculous numbers of white pieces
To end the story like a deus ex snow machine but since the snow has no eyes
She could not see you plugging in your loom I'll call you tomorrow.

JERRY'S SMOG, BLAKE'S FEET

There is a goddess of the pass and valley, a wet one,
to see her
take that rag away from your face.

The hills were clouded in the usual yellow smoke,
you were crying, sort of, from bad air and rapture,
not the goddess dead, no arrows glancing off our speeding wet metal.
It's only the carbon cycle, ashes to et cetera and dust to et cetera,
and the autos' breath.

Take that rag away from your face.
The fog in a populated valley
is pieces of the buried,
milky fumes from the lawns,
grace in hard nuts sucked up from branches,
cracked in the clouds,
everything that mixes with the ocean in the clouds
now that are moistening our big ghostly car,
fog in a populated valley.

What to do but breathe?
Whose diaphanous breath on the windshield,
whose funky wet garment
in gray folds near your nose?

Well, while Blake in 1804 asked for his chariot,
which he did not have,
his bow, his spear,

which he didn't have either,
here, in this "Valley of Smoke," their aboriginal name,
autoless and aboriginal they lay face down in the dirt for hours
presumably to feel better or while away the hours.
The goddess visited them to help but they were very rustic,
naked and consumed with fad of lying face down in dirt.
For hours she beat the fog upon them in waves:
". . . it is so moist, so cool, turn to me."
They hardly moved, a dozen buttocks up in a field,
she dissolved her body to a heavy, sweet gas
and sent it over the field like arrows of desire,
but they hardly moved, a dozen in a field,
then she re-formed herself,
the goddess panting and sweating.

Upon the tops of the dripping Australian bushes
imported and planted around these dark satanic homes,
we'll look for the sun.
It comes at noon or one every day,
my visitor. It doesn't fail, so get ready,
wipe the ecstasy from your eyes,
give me my grapefruit over there, a burning gold ball to throw.
It's on the seat.
Australian tears in the fog, white Chryslers in the street.

CORRESPONDENTS

DEAR WIND

When you shiver like a person
From spraying in all directions day or night your forces
Like our iron country becoming threads in the sun or our
Universe, get this, exploding as usual, stars mere shrapnel,
Moons splinters, the planet a fragment surrounded by a breeze,
In short, when you tremble and aren't sick, don't worry,
I know a steady luminous person
Who knows the generation's central idea
Which is simple, acute, and makes you feel good: here, imagine
Wind doesn't exist, never invented, and I told you
Sails are its statues and its great vegetables
As in cauliflower much larger, flatter, and smoother
Or an unframed supple mural depicting white's shades
And so are firemen's backfires its antidote to burning.
I like the rain in manifold slabs of density or fineness
Layered in the space across the valley after the vicious fires of October
Especially soaking that brittle grass for which there is no hope but you
       don't care.
Fickle and powerful, but not like people, like first light, so much
Bouncing off lots of hydrogen no one could see in that translucency.

LETTER TO WIND ABOUT MY HOUSE

October gone, fire-black steep canyons drenched
Over there, poor coyotes dead, here my three friends the phones
Calling like pets that interrogative noise like "please"—

Can't you hear them in their beds called "hooks"—
So that when they exhaust themselves
Through the thin silence my clean, kept plants versus nature's
Which are under an exhaust-smoke sky
Surge at the ceiling, thicken, and are happy.
In the mild hills against my windows
An animal unseen in folds of ivy
Digs a home—the dirt sifts and rattles down the leaves all day.
Will he be black and white and incredibly strong
In my L.A. County trap?
Bushes, beasts, you name it,
The external world in its entirety is all around me out here.
It's night now, at the house's side on my loose tiles
Something the size of me is walking but don't be afraid.

See his slit, yellow eyes and gentle demeanor?
Giant dog in the Hollywood hills.

DOME AND CAVE—POEM TO WIND

Heaven, your hat, began to seem self-effacing, for it.
It was no more than some ideal countryside—
Cool woods, hot ocean, a natural fresh pool,
And an all-purpose store hidden in a ravine
With anonymous, efficient city clerks who don't ingratiate themselves.
Hell, your pavement, began to seem not too bad at first,
A house with a tricky stove, the need for luck on the highway,
Months of the dentist, death decades away, or perhaps all of this at once.
This is why on the transcontinental phone Norman and myself
Repeat great fire on the whole earth, a plague of senility and low IQ,
Government attacking Phoenix and Philadelphia,
And feel close, like friends, because we know this'll happen in 1990 to '95.

Suppose my wife and I couldn't make money?
Suppose we had kids?
Suppose we didn't?
I swear to you, a very great bird
Will come over that patio from beyond those hills,
Coyotes dripping from his mouth, and carry me to you.
Soon, OK?

TWO

INSIDE OUT

THE PICTURE

In this one, we sat on the floor.
Beyond the thin glass the idea of water and thunder
Was like a seizure in God's mind
("Fresher! Fresher!" he yelled, and threw the water down)
And among our legs which smelled like salt and blood
We spread out the thousand photographs,

A few aunts dead, the Cartier-Bresson imitations we published,
Our cats at two months, that auditorium
Where we saw Lowell eight years ago deserted
Afterward so in our frame it looked like erosion
In a waterless desert or a hill so steep
You'd think at a sneeze someone would have somersaulted down
Over body after body into his sidekick poet
Rich's lap. The old girl friends,
The boys who had you, in snapshots
Somehow better than the 8 x 10s we were secretly so proud of and sold.

In nearly every one, of us,
There's this irony on my face and always on yours
That keeps us from being scared
At the nervelike blue light which instant by instant attacks the powerful rain
At the edge of the window.
                    There's a smile
In one of them that makes you look like the sweetest shark ever
And as I pass it to you a gagging cloud makes us a little nervous.
There's even some spectacular ones of a robbery—I can still hear the guns!—
And under the roof of your bare, crossed legs whiter than surf

The expensive, quiet-shuttered camera we've just dusted off
Seems ready to wink cahoots at the storm.
                                    Near it
A color shot of my aunt crying because she'll die. Near
That, a second one in color that friends took last week
—we still seem to be in our twenties—
And we can by now look openly and decently at someone's lens.

Cover these awful two with your leg and I'll come closer.
We'll grin at the window when the blue light electrocutes it.

SWOLLEN SONNET

We've wanted to see a strange animal
Suddenly come upon in a parking lot at the edge of a little phony woods.
I've studied this for five years; it is likely to be a wolf
Which will seem like a much larger, leaner, shaggier German shepherd.
Look me in the eyes in the car, just a small turn
Of the shoulders, OK? Since all honesty disappears
In a methodical, protracted search for a strange animal,
I love birds with fierce nylon masks and cheaply dyed feathers.
You love the swift truly ugly fish of the cold ridiculously deep waters,
Their flesh so densely packed there are no air spaces in the body
And no eyes that would be weak spots in life in the absolute dark.
So are we those animals of gravity and light
That cruise above the highways shutting off cars?
Soon they'll be seen by a thousand reliable humans at once,
And we won't be there, I swear to you—
Desires in our pack of two are like an ocean of black asphalt nine miles deep,
Thickness nature never heard of and oh here you are across this little lot;

I start the engine and rev it,
You stop halfway and are staring at me.

MY SHOES

Tarzan refreshed. He completely emptied his mind for two minutes
lying in underbrush; not even "rhinoceros" the word
remained. His open hibernated eyes looked for snakes and other
jungle effluvia. I'd settle for that power if I could also
be handsome like a slightly chubby blonde folksinger. And
my non-publisher likes my snide
frivolous tone but not enough he calls
to say. O to be in *your* shoes! Is to be in El
Greco's to see leaky El Grecos everywhere all the time? To
be in Tarzan's! *You* are eating. You have an
idea, a complete idea, which is satisfying. You tell me. You
chew. The phone rings, we don't answer. That's *simplicity*!
uncompounded! But to be in America in 1142, circumcised
and smart as a whip! Or to phone and say! Hello, this is
the President, President Vogelsang, here's how I really
see things. But I don't want to be like anyone
who wants to be brilliant and powerful and good. I want to fake
simplicity and have you call me Mr. El Intricate
in a house filled with perfect rubber costumes.

That one of me, filled, does what you do;
your empty one is on the phone giving my name.

HERE, THERE

Sun oranged out behind small black hills,
Extending funny light for hours.
Snow fell fell and fell.
Alone at last, fake children
Off with huge ugly wife to see *Blow-Up* again,
I put on my Phantom suit, lit a Camel, squinted,
Felt old trauma of being father at fifteen pass,
And thought for a long time about my animals, the dog
As fast as the horse, both loyal and vicious.
In false light, nubile bodies crunched past
One storey below my low window. So I stood,
Raised one of my twin automatics,
And click click clicked some,
Cursing price of ammo.
Objects like furniture in room bounced stuff into my eyes.
Only light I guess, though
Curtain chair wall slammed into eyes too.
I finished a letter to be mimeographed
For my friends and enemies:
"Sam our child gave Bob our child
Bronchitis in the summertime in hateful New York
But keen air here cured them."
Damn them, damn them all.
Eyes continued to collide with (without
Marring) the furniture, without ripping
The rug, or cracking the mirror.
Small skinny pretty wife by herself
Opened front door and stood in lamplight saying

This living room is camp and hateful New York
And I said Since the snow is bouncing and spilling into
The other uninhabited
Falsely white-lit three rooms, they are
Antarctica, Antarctica, and Antarctica.

TORNADO READING IN THE MORNING

No little clouds six feet by three scudding
along the ceiling.
Even air in all the rooms of the house.
Outside this would be un
natural.
While vicious tapered clouds hurry
and tumble to make the announcer's
voice stumble every May so I shut him off
and plan an appropriate spur-of-the-moment gift for you.
Unlike, how can I say?—nature?—every
gift changes: Dr. Spock's paperback book crawls
up the wall, across the ceiling. That
gift should be a funny book-shaped box of animal crackers, one
among them the inch-long featureless foetus.
Never opened! Unlike the well-thumbed
Rachel Carson book about poison with the
glass of ice water making a slowly spreading
warp on it. Coming in for lunch
in May in Kansas when I
point in that direction saying "There's
a gift for you," you drink the water
that's poisoning the gift. Sirens
interrupt my consideration of *Modern European Poetry*.
A typical poem in it considers whether
the siren has become the storm or the storm still is,
ridiculous to you who dream of really
flying in a room full of people.

So I'll give you this joke:
For fun I say seriously
Now don't get frightened but some very tiny clouds
have come in the house and are bouncing along the ceiling
like smoky balloons. It gets you for an instant,
the short sound from your throat is applause
that comes down the street and kisses the living room
like a nudge.

EDITING AT HOME
WITH A SICK WOMAN

Doggy-breath, I gulp more coffee, gulp more,
lean into my RUSH ms. The author warns
against pouring oneself into the volatile compound
at this point. I giggle, scribble, and write over.
Smacking an orange, my new girl shushes me,
a wet, bitchy whistle,
and stares into a real chemistry book.
For five days she's her own diuretic,
caffeine's mine, and she's my sour diurnal flower.

Cramped aide in my big green robe, she bends to see,
citrus breath cutting my air.
"It's easy, it's the formula for salt
compared to the formula for the ocean
with two typos." I can't ignore
her smirking pungent swirl
back to the couch to cut another orange,
the glass plate grating and screeching.

I rearrange more words and think of a kiss.
"Coffee and acid must curdle," I say out loud.
Wavy robed, she pours into the bedroom.
Human catalyst, I make the author's last sentence clear
but unchanged—that's the trick.

I've let my lips into my cup
so many times they are two warm thighs.

My mouth is soft dank brass.
Her kiss is a knife squeaking through caked blood.

DOLLY OUT

I pick the acetate out of my stomach
Sprocket, for lack of an image write my non
Publisher, throw her bra and lens
Cleaning tissue off my desk, get the hot
Dogs out for dinner, and curse roaches and my grand
Parents. I still covet grandfather's twenties movie
Money that he lost in the you
Know what but I sickened of going to student
Union films that checked with the clippings grand
Mother handed me on her death
Sofa and I tired of haunting the flickering TV after mid
Night. My hopeless little lover tunnels
Into Brooklyn shooting blacks with her handy
Bolex and snidely fucks grand
Father whenever I bring him
Up. He brought from Germany to Cali
Fornia a scaffold with tracks
Up into the air, along the air, and so for the first
Time the camera moved with the action.
Grandfather and grandmother moved with the action
To the tune of three million bucks one year.
The lack of a recognizable image or a voice
Ran actors, poets, and camera
Men into Brooklyn on rails before.
So what. Purity
Is what we want when we're dirty
And money when we're poor.
Fame from rhymed sour grapes is worth settling for.

THE SINGER

Music was harder than coming
Among those hills in May and leaning
On one, I remember, you opened your hand
And said look, all I'm trying to play
Is a foreground of cataclysmic darkness
Behind which can be seen a glimmer of light
On this adequate guitar . . . see?

I shut up like the inadequate valves of my hands
But leaned harder on the hill which I saw
Squinting through my fist
As a brush held like a thick stick by a painter
In an immense bright blue smock with round
Puffy white hands that drifted slowly over the whole canvas.
A blob of yellow shook on the brush like steel mashed into paint.

The brush was the hill. The painter was the sky.
The clouds were his hands at the edge of the hill,
Which stroked the shivering yellow paint
Which was your guitar. The day squeezed closed,
Opening the night, which hummed simply black, black.

THE NIGHT

Through the window the moon shone on the table so hard
We once in a while shielded our eyes
While we told from our lives stories that broke small
Bones in our toes, sent you crying to another room
Only to return to tell something that popped my nipple
Across the table, making a sudden sharp rise in my shirt, a
Small bloodstain. Another story bent my thumbs back and made
Us cough for air. Then we made one up together:
He painted his way to a Hollywood party, then another,
And spread rumors that he was the champion foreplay
Artist. I heard it's really different, people would say.
His best painting went on and on, an accordion-like
Cardboard mural with 225 scenes, the first painting ever
Made into a movie. *She* had a photographic
Memory, her car was sworn in by extraterrestrials
One day, with them she chased something no
One ever heard of, she was as ripe as those new
Tomatoes bred in the shape and size of a small hard sharp pin,
Besides that, she was famous, rich, and talented, and she
Had a *giant* clitoris. They met. The moon passed off the edge
Of the table, we examined ourselves for cuts or bruises,
But the surfaces of our arms, thighs, foreheads, chests, were
Unblemished, soft, straight, and perfect, as if for over a quarter
Of a century they had not been dipped in the round pocked hard moon.

FEELING THAT WAY TOO

It gets dark and I get scared.
Dogs bark, stop, and bark continuously,
The only sound
As the plunging sun chars orange clouds
In what seems to be Nevada.
You are afraid too and go into the bedroom to sleep
Clothed under blankets in corduroys and wool socks,
Bare chest probably cool.
Our cats blink at me, raise and let limp their heads.
Disturbed too, you heave a little and rustle.
The bed creaks and squeaks seconds after.
I still sit still, monitoring the blood in my ears.
And suppose, though shivering with fright, I *should*
Dance in the pale dark, waving my pants
Over my head, singing I've got bells
That jingle jangle jingle or Pepsi-Cola
Hits the spot? Or switch a light on?
The moon fills up its ugly red cheeks as
Silence comes down like a hunk
Of gooey lead in the ear.
And though a few seconds later you will say
"Oh I feel so good, my bare skin feels so nice, like ice cream,"
Now I hear you walking through the dark hall
Then naked you step quickly through a white beam
In this room then hurry to me in that six-foot wide shaft
Of total blackness between the beam and me and
My eyes tear and I really do reach for the switch.

THE COMPANION

Because I was funny and hard
A far more well-known woman artist than I myself
Ate with me and angrily and casually
In a large, bright restaurant told me of the gifts of darkness
Of her brother Van Gogh, his intent
That the howling, misc. red dripping, and rage
Of ancient life would appear in all future art in all
Its (the howling's) completeness and abundancy.
That he realized that if this black surge were successful,
And also if the deep white being
That was frightening her in spots in her paintings
As she herself tried the same thing, were to emerge widespread
In, say, 1997, it would work against Picasso and against everyone,
Me, the buses' many heads framed in glass rows that go by our table,
Against the President and the waiter,
And that furthermore it might turn out that she was wrong,
Her consciousness split, like a camel (carrying five leather pouches
Of ideas instead of two and miles gone)
Will fall in the sand, four legs spread out in four directions.

It was me who said the part about the camel.
Beyond the range of hills shadowing the lovely restaurant in gray
Was a desert, and that helped me think of it.
Her face was powerful
Like a boxer's shoulder but was also like a woman's genital
When you are disposed to connect it with heart-rending beauty.
Though we then drank and gossiped, white streaks of laughter,
I was frightened for two weeks. I guess nobody's self-sufficient,

Though some paintings are, like those of her brother Picasso,
But it was me who said the part about the buses' rows of framed heads,
And it was me who interjected howling, awful dripping, and rage,
And it was me who thought of an existence too deep and too bright,
It was me, me, me.

THREE

CLASHES

THE CLOUDS

I am smoking Camels and crying
This activity is helping me think of clouds like white
Cool bathroom porcelain in a rich friend's house
It is 1:08 A.M. in my nice back room in Wichita in late December 1972
And Paul Carroll's book The Poem in Its Skin which sadly enough
I am not in is already be
Come reactionary and a bit bitchy to
Night our President is taking no
Shit one he is tamping about one-third of his power
Into the throats of unfair journalists two he is devoting
Much of his day to the number one bombing
Raid forever in all history since about 1970 we
Have bought a color TV which we can't afford and I will very carefully
Watch football in two days no smoking cig
Arettes I hate, no perusing powerful poetry
Books between plays three the President is right about the TV
Blackouts of the redskins Washingtonians won't
See their game unless they go to Camp David and pick
It up from Pennsylvania he is trying
To do something about all this and I am in unrequited
Love with clouds in Wichita dragging deeply on powerful cigarettes
What a shit I must be they are not even
Clouds no wonder Paul Carroll didn't take any
Of my poems for his truly fabulous but not very powerful on a global scale
Anthology The Young American Poets suppose white clouds
Of the white I described in the second and third lines were
Over the entire earth
"Blanketing" it like a cliché

Now this minute we wouldn't know because of
The fucking dark night so I hate the night quite a bit
But it is my love for the clouds
Which makes me cry and smoke Camels off
And on to 1:35 A.M. the time
Of composition from line 4 to this line it is
Not Frank O'Hara's death or the poking things Paul
Carroll says about him in his book © 1968 it is not the brave
Things on p. 258 and 259 I read Robert Bly
Does I go to the refrigerator and smoke and drip
In it it is very white my wife Judy who I love
Has casually cleaned it after coming home from directing the local lead-ins to
News of President Nixon's activities the door is chillier than cool I stop
Crying and release the faucet's steady bright gray water onto my Camel

But if as I plan to do one can calmly drink a beer to sleep soundly
To wake to write very real clouds in endlessly sunny days
Does one?

DEER HERD BRINGS PUMA TO KANSAS

A F O U N D P O E M

Riding in my house
Whose interior varied details such as furniture
Have been smoothed featureless by
Riding in the clouds,
The newspaper comes, claims
A few pair of puma do reside
Inside the state and growing deer
Herds probably will attract more.
Dr. Arthur Zoom of Kansas State University
Claims there are at least two pair of the big cats
In the Blue River area near the Nebraska line.
Zoom has casts of cat tracks
Identified as those of four large puma.
These casts, Zoom says, resemble clouds.

Reports have come in repeatedly
Over the past twelve years
About two of the big predator cats
Being seen northwest of Washington, Kansas,
And one pair was seen south of Manhattan
On one occasion and again last fall
Near Council Grove, Zoom said.
As they run through nearby fields they look like clouds, Zoom said.

Wichitan Al Shot reported to Zoom
That signs of puma including tracks and distant sightings
Have been long prevalent
In the Ninnescah River area.

Shot is a bow hunter who stalks big game
In a several-state area. He has a
Colorado mountain lion (a term interchangeable with "puma")
To his bow hunting credit. When Zoom visited Shot's home,
The puma lying on the floor
Appeared to Zoom for quite a while to be a cloud.

Zoom said another pair of puma, the nation's biggest cat,
Are known to wander the Parsons-Coffeyville area,
While a pair in the Burlington vicinity
Have been seen repeatedly.
The animals probably followed deer along stream banks
From Colorado originally, and now that the Kansas deer herd
Is sizable, they may multiply within the state.
Deer and smaller wild animals
Are their main fare though they have been known
To attack domestic animals.
Zoom reports that when he was visiting a farm
A few years ago, two large puma ambushed
A cow in a nearby meadow, and all three animals in the meadow
Looked like clouds tumbling across the sky.

Authenticated sighting of the puma
Is rare, Zoom explained,
Because the cat is very timid about coming near
Any point of human activity
And because it so resembles a cloud. Game officers
Have been unable to find any of the big cats
In areas where excited residents contend
The puma has visited, and there is little doubt
Some of the reports of tracks and livestock vandalism
Attributed to the puma are created by other wildlife

Including the bobcat, feral dogs, and human thieves.
Because of this, Zoom advises that hunters and farmers
Give a warning shout if they cannot make a clear
Identification. Clouds and bullets mix
But you may not want to shoot a thief, he says.

A LITTLE CRAZY

You are sad. You are leaning down on
your sadness like the rain is trying to do to us
but we are in the house. You are
watching the water fall so easily from the
tap, you are whizzing through the dishes, you are a man
sweating in the next room in a few minutes
when a woman wants to do it in
the middle of the day, in the middle of her
body, you are encouraging the rain with a subtle
fierceness and it is doing it as fast as it can,
you are saying lines from movies in a negro
dialect but your tongue sticks to the
roof of your mouth, you are thinking of your younger
possible girl friends, strangers on the
street who make their stomachs hard to barely press
by, you are thinking of the unusualness
of raining hard, there is a terrible drought
coming in a few hundred years, your
state is becoming a desert quarter
inch by quarter inch, everything
is turning into Florida's sadness when it rains
and the water stands around and the natives pray
the ground to sop it up and you go out
and the dry heat from the high blue aching sky
meets your sadness ten feet above the ground
and you run back in the house to take a poison shower.

CORRESPONDENCES

They think lies are just curly clichés
and when so many are curled
blondly around a body, that's
just a personality, perhaps even of a
friend. Or that's a huge meat
sandwich or a rose and if they fall all over it it's
wet. If those aren't tears, you're supposed to call it rain.
You are thinking you are roses or blonde
or both, it's the nice warm air of
January in which Snow, the Lie,
is sliding from tricky roofs like your friends
are from you. Then the next day it's zero-gray
and hard and everyone is happy to fall
in different perfect pieces
whitely on the world and cover it. But you are
roses, or blonde, and must lie in silence beside
your own phone like a 160-lb. deep image
with ears so anhydrous they respond to no human bell, like
a mailman so pledged to his profession he
never receives messages, always hears hi from Chicago
behind his back, or dearest from Phoenix,
as toward the next house
he does not open the next letter. Aching
you are from crying to the summer to peel
away your hot beauty lie by lie leaving
you open and blonde to them again.

CHRISTMAS, 1968; SISTER, 13

At seven A.M. most winter sun
over the semi-tropical canal
bores a fuzzy channel through amazing fog
to make us feel warmer than Florida.
Jane, is your coffee? virgin desire's focus
in this brightest-gray, evenest light?
to your musty mouth, morning tongue?
Star ships stick in the throat.

At least the TV tends to pastels.
I don't think my eye's diaphragm shuts much further.
You don't play with the blinds or the Tint,
you ask questions, harder and harder.
No, I don't suppose it is much like
my 707 yesterday. Yes, they can't say they're lonely, yes,
we are spinning at thirty-three miles a minute,
yes, I am excited. The soft, round sun
breathes on David, Chet, the astronauts, you, and me,
and parents, wife, and the town are asleep.
The crocodile you've seen in the canal about ten steps away
sleeps under wet glass. Braving the morning
to fly to the moon with my little sister,
shocking awake my tired, unmonitored body for love of her,
the fat round machine we ride is not engineered
and I hate the shinier and shinier sun eating the fog
to show telephone poles, expensive houses, gas stations,
and bring out the family to ask how far they've gone now.

POEM

Sometimes if you've been in and out of them a lot for you
The clouds and layers of air and color become stale.
They can boil and twist, spill blood on the plane,
Or tilt like a hundred soft long mirrors,
All you want is intelligent vicious arguments,
Or a peaceful cluttered room where you're busy and powerful,
If only to you. Or exposing sunsets to laughter!
How obvious that long silver idiot is lying on those mountains.

While the soul is our creation, anyway I take care of mine,
And if once in a while it wants to be famous and petty
I want that too or like it a pornographic movie by day,
Falling asleep over the *Aeneid* with friends by night.

I guess sunsets are death and dawn is a birth
You can be sure about like a rebirth or the feeling of renewal
Vegetables get from shit but the soul is the sun itself that hammers on all.

POEM

It's the famous sun. Between buildings
Whose sides are yellow emotion
It is roaring force and pigeons
Head toward it in their sad, mediocre arcs.

You come into the city crying a little.
You let loose the wet past
And think of the assholes who would tremble
When your big ugly wings raised your shirt

And ripped it. And saying, Good-bye jerks, up you'd go
In a heartless spiral heavenward
As you think of loving explosions alone
And your two tears dry and it gets very quiet.

SITTING AT HOME

(THINKING OF THIS)

Seven people look at the wall. A large piece of saranwrap
Like a slice of the world hangs there
And in pastels on it is a smokestack
And the blue Philadelphia sky.

Outside a man climbs the side of their building.
He is pop-eyed and looks in
The window which the people shrug
At as just a painting that's come alive.

The man is not the event of the day.
Phones are ringing, many small streams
Of blood fall to the floor from between the 3,000 sheets of paper
They must deal with. On one shelf

A tiny (3-in.-high) man is hysterically
Speaking Spanish, making demands. This is their normal day.
So the man with the powerful eyes invents someone,
Beams him, you know, through the saranwrap window

Into a chair which is also invented
Or eyeballed into the room. The people greet the new man,
Actually a woman, and soon they all know her,
They know how she eats and how she talks to her husband.

Once at cocktail hour in that room she tells them that Homer's
Great poem was like a transparent curtain

(Figures struggling in and out of the fiber)
Which divided the language of beasts

From the language of invention
And they disagree and lift her up wriggling toward that wall and window.

A PACKAGE OF MAGAZINES

While your slave whacks away
In your yard in Ngorongoro
Eliminating the trespassing banana tree,
That bunch of littles from the States
You are shuffling in your big big hands
Like 52 cards confidently under the mini-torrented fan.

You haven't changed into your cheetah suit
To hunt the stupid, blood-filled Kansas squirrel at 4 A.M.
For a month for a very good reason
Which you can't figure out which you
Are looking for in these pages. It's so hard. You
Look out the window and it's Africa! no wonder! It's

Still morning and your slave gets the giggles
From thinking of when you came out to pick a banana
He saw your whole body shiver
From realizing how cool, delicious, and lonely
A cool, delicious, and lonely African morning can be.

You watch his skin keep his ice in. Can you alter
Your supernatural powers to change
Into a slave suit instead of a cheetah suit
And have you already?
Of course desperately you thumb through those books again.

PRESENTLY

I was going to have outdoor lunch with a man who had studied carpentry
And classical piano and I was afraid of him;
No outlaw stance of mine would make an impression, nothing I was
Would interest him, though of course I had something he wanted,
Information, advice. He regretted in advance that it would have to be
A short, quick lunch and thinking of that which was short
But not quick and the quick that wasn't short, in other words
With a vague acute hostility I hid behind people in the street
And observed him approach, sit at "our" table, and become impatient.
Time passed. There is a later, when I got mine, but this is how people
Are now, him and me, when each human spirit advances regardless,
And this means you.

THE PALACE AT THE HEARST RANCH

Few could swim in the thirties
So the deep indoor pool of many electric moons, the best,
With Pompeiian mosaic tile dating to 60 B.C.,
Was left for wranglers and gardeners
And their angular muscled women who had
Leverage in their too-long thighs and had white, crooked teeth.

Outside was a shallow black-tiled pool, bigger even,
Surrounded by Italian marble goddesses
And the front fragment of a Roman temple,
Where Clark, Buster, and dozens like them
Goofed off and held serious conversations wet to the chest.
Screen goddesses with usual bodies and heavenly faces
Let their agents do their talking, while they themselves must have
Been the ones who drew the moon closer to the earth.

Between the pools tonight the intellectual porker Hearst
Goes back and forth, dripping, high on wine, following up a hill
And mocking an anonymous actor hired to mime Arthur Rimbaud
Who goes back and forth limping on 1½ legs in Victorian clothes.
Chaplin follows them and at once limps like the fake Rimbaud
And like Hearst mock-limping. At the edge of each pool
The Rimbaud dives well and fully clothed swims in a slight semicircle
Toward the other end, then Hearst dives beautifully, a fat Olympian,
And easily passes the 1½-legged, fully clothed Rimbaud. Charlie
Hesitates, as he would surely drown in deep water, then
Stands still and begins to cheer,
A sound like eight people cheering,

Then the wranglers, gardeners, and their sinewy women
Begin to cheer. This happens twice at each pool; they are separated
By a gentle hill two hundred yards long.
At the famous guests' pool, the three limpers stand at one end
To an ovation.
                    The Rimbaud hesitates, motionless.
The audience of stars standing in water is breathless, quiet—
Pink, wigged statues in the water.

I do not know if the anonymous actor was a Socialist
And wanted to lead everyone to the other pool to mix,
Or simply had bad timing. But he stood there too long,
Hearst dove long and shallow like a fat arrow,
And Chaplin walked around toward his agent in a normal gait,
The walk of a mailman, which some were shocked to see.

I cannot tell you The Rimbaud was a ghost of Arthur.
Oh yes, the brightness of the moonlight was frightening.
Thalberg was afraid of it, as were others.
What would *you* do if you were a bad actor in that spot?
Then sudden floating laughter from *each* pool about other subjects
As if life went on regardless
Or as if there were two souls, not one, slowly
Plunging into each other for hours.
Why should men die?

FOUR

COMPASS

LETTER TO SHAKESPEARE

We live longer, space and time are pale and relative
And are often not hunky and not dory for instance in jet lag,
Or when the thought of death or parting makes love black
With which you're familiar, listen

Imagine riding the airplane or a muscular gliding bird with big lungs.
Below, a speedboat on limitless water (that must be the ocean)
Digs deep into water, I'm in the boat, an electric horn (a wire hangs from it)
On which must be my voice is shouting up to you

And you can't hear this because of your engines
Around you, or the bird's athletic breathing at each stroke,
The wind in his feathers, the wind in your ears, or your fear.
Gradually as in classical music which always makes me sad

I will continue forever in such water with such a boat and horn
And sometimes a big strong bird or plane overhead.
Help me, Shakespeare
                   to turn to the land mass

(Turn around) so close behind, see it?
Which is such a monster hunk of land
You can cross it only in what I've called an airplane
Or furtively via death when your loved one on its other side

Appears here on your eyeballs.
For instance, I'm looking out an open window in LA while

Countless little airplanes flutter around hills far away in the sunshine
Making me sleepy and almost late for my cab (taxicab).

Now I'm sure there is a great plane waiting for me:
I can see its images, pale or black, rising and sinking in the sky.

THE RADIO,
THE NORTON ANTHOLOGY

Yeah it's somewhat late
Teens and hillbillies are racing old family cars
(That sound like the surface of the sun)
And I'm a-sittin aroun a-thinkin of threnody.

Pop pop the moon passes
Thru some stuff in space undiscovered as yet
(Dotting the announcer's euphemistic news of)
The phantom wooer
A powerful blonde woman
Who fucks you first and then kills you dead
Be you girl or boy—
"She's zipping thru the city air at electronic speed,
Listener, just a-aimin for the top floor of your house. . . ."
(She must know I'm sitting here tonight
Thinking of threnody.)

Southey wrote "The Three Bears."
History is dealing harshly also
With those obnoxious kids. Goldilocks, whom they've picked up,
Is frenchkissing them and burning their tongues
With hot soup from the side of her mouth.

Marconi's S went around the world, shot off the
Planet's edge, and came back 13 years later
Stronger than if just bounced off something. God's
Backhand, the announcer says, and I hear

The cat burglar turned out to be a slim, blonde lady.
In the dark in the dark in the kitchen
She crept around stealing people's Campbell's soup
Then getting in bed with their kids
On moonless dark moonless nights.

(It is in the morning the misty morn ya ya
That I know I will realize things have happened all day
On the lit half of the earth
while the weak China sun applause noise
Applause noise

PROLETARIAT

In the brain there is an LA and an NYC,
There's blue veins like those on your breasts and there's an AV:
On the street, à la concrete and glass canyons,
There are the millions, myth of worth swarming,
And a poet honing his humility
In language that's no language nor as beautiful.

Ambiguity sandwiches and simple childhood desires
On every block, loneliness heavy in red American Flyer wagons,
The sane running frontways then sideways pulling them.
This is in the city and in the brain.

Out West for fifty cents in any corner's machine, a map of the heart—
Careful—multicolored—numbers of all the citizens' houses
Each one, and the shapes of water-cut canyons
Charted in *feet* are shapes liké white rose petals on the paper.

I argue bitterly with loved ones on the coasts,
Insulting each other's dignity but not our intelligence—
We're trembling and we're smart to tremble, there's
In the countless skulls around us the spiralling coils of DNA
And we shout as was the Indian custom when afraid
Of John Smith's map of wherever they'd been and what still wasn't there.

AUGUST, N. LINN ST.

Storms averaged two hours, fat
Hours heavy with extra minutes.
Two women were alone in the poem about Iowa City
In Iowa City itself ha ha. They
Were beautiful, weren't they, as they smoked cigarettes
And walked under the jungle-like trees
In the middle afternoon? In the town.
The somewhat personless town
Was green as you stood,
Wherever you stood, like green water deep over the roofs,
And they were smart, they
Were walking fast, they were baring
Their emotions and laughing like laughter
Was the beautiful penis that broke all hearts.
A friend says this happened.
                              "I was miserable,"
One of the women told him, "we both were,
So we took a walk." The bar's diabolical clock (a
Local myth) was slow a half hour every afternoon
Then caught up
Or that afternoon quietness raised its own skirt
When the rain came onto the street like a loud silly car
And in the hollow uninhabited dark bar
They told him this, even how the previous rain,
In the morning, swelled and warped the day.
I don't know which.
The story is so embellished by now
That the women wear shorts and are crying, smoking,
And moving along under the trees.

YOKING

Damaged slightly by a cyclone, on a day I changed my life,
Were in front of me two paintings by Paul Gauguin, House of Delight,
And one other, a masterpiece, L'Appel, The Call.
You will understand there was
At my desk a sexy Polaroid of an aunt slightly beyond my age
At her death, but ripe and condescending when I asked for it back
For those terrific legs spread slightly.
Unlike sad vapor climbing upward fast in storms
A good boy's lascivious glances are happy enough today,
She isn't bitter anymore up there in the fleecy clouds.
This writ at my desk, the sun
Came around in back of me while I was in the building,
Thinking this. You who I have tried so hard to make my friend
Sit still once, glance casually not too hard
At the buildings drenched across the way
Which show this is a day once too bright becoming night—
As masterpieces are simple, there's no reason for the concrete to be pink,
There's no reason for the sand and water to be pink.
Imagine, "damaged by a cyclone" said about these two pieces of paper,
Or waking in a house that smelled like straw, soil, the mildewed canvas
Of uncle's green duffel bag from the Pacific war.

POEM

Here on Mars, it's simple.
It's clear. Books, horses, and straight screwing
Go from left to right as in real life
And the weather is a sponge storm every time. About that
There's no confusion in newspapers and there are heights, low
Hills and ridiculous, breathtaking mountains,
Like the knockers of a very big angel,
And you can shoulder through bold mist
Feeling silly and small; it's not painful. Here if you don't say
What you feel you'll go mad
Rave into the bushes
And every so often I give a poor person change, when I'm on Mars.
It's simultaneous like harmony, it's sane.

It's tragic like a peripeteia dust storm.
And this tragedy is more intricate and beautiful
Than even the dust arranging itself in soft throbs in columns
Miles high as one elaborate grotesque woman
Like women is an enigma without pants and is
Demanding motions at cross purposes from her lover
And the fog is not easy it's as hard as gravity
Sadness in barrels by the side of the road for the cured
Who go into the translucent woods
To pray to the black heart of betrayal to blend them into the black trees
This is how it always is,
While you speak you understand.

A TOUR OF "CIVILISATION"
AT THE WICHITA ART MUSEUM

FOR JON AND JUDY

FROM THE CATALOGUE: *"The works loaned to this
exhibition . . . are arranged in the thirteen eras
proposed by Sir Kenneth Clark in the 'Civilisation'
film series. In some instances, for the purposes of
this exhibition, works are not strictly chronologically
arranged. The suit of armor, for example, utilized
in the section 'Romance and Reality,' serves to
illustrate the battle attire of the Crusades, yet it
dates in fact from the sixteenth century."*

I'm nervous all the time and history is steady.

    In a soup bowl of blood
    Teeny Vikings rowed and yawped away,
    Pulleys attached to their oars
    And to a flywheel which turned the generator
    For my electric typewriter
    With which I kept their log
    As I chewed my gum
    And recorded their proofs of the undulatory theory of light.
    Our guide lifted a leg,
    Gave it a twang,
    And it shivered like a tuning fork.
    "That's what I mean by demon
    In the blood," she said,
    "And it was things like that and TB
    That they tried to let drip out
    Into this blood bowl."

It's the female children who scream like they're coming,
The man lying in his motel bed thought
As he snapped his gum and thought of heaven too,
Who make cold, electrified motel pools so noisy and so bright
And make the best women later.
Accidentally he discovered
Such fake history
Came from his personality
And made her shake
Like a loose tooth
Embedded in the wall
For a switch.

The king himself bent down
To retrieve her stocking
And her red shoe
With which she painted and made her leg twang.
He did it because she was a goddess
Because she could paint and twang with a red shoe
And with a stocking
As in a whadda-ya-call-it . . . a happening.

"The most out-of-the-way most minor
Period in painting, the most lacking in visual conception,
Was Tuesday afternoon when that gentleman in the back there . . ."
(She pointed near me)
". . . turned his eyes from the sky
To Darvon and Wrigley's
Because of his gasping, flashy migraine," she said.

Religious models wore the rich clothes of their own day,
Their tits hanging out against a very real sky

And Pluto's very sinews and foreskin and soft balls
She stubbornly stood for against our giggles,
"For though such things are funny to you," she said,
"They show the smooth flow of the race's
Focus of attention from heaven—"
Which the man in the motel room is thinking about
As he gently holds his gum between his tongue and his front teeth—
"To this life, these muscles, that organ, those glands
Flopping flopping out."

Everything is chronological except showing off,
Shaking the salt
Into the shaker
Perfectly, the top on, one grain for each hole,
Which could be a particular
Way of seducing the guide.

    "We can't talk about it yet
    Because it's not history
    It's not digested and ready to flow into the blood
    Besides it's frightening as hell
    Without the distance which makes it cute
    I mean op and pop and the surreal and cubism
    Which some of you may have heard of
    And which we can chew so to speak but not yet swallow."

Now Jon and Judy
You'll think this is funny and has shape
Because to you my personality is a flickering field of study:
That afternoon I asked her to go to a motel and see
Me pour with one tip of the hand
Fifteen single grains of salt into the fifteen

Holes of the shaker.
Each one a swish.
No noise of salt tapping plastic
Until the grains hit bottom.
She thought of the parallel instantly
And whipped off her skinny stockings.
After a shocking swim which charged us up
She went all the way:
She lay in one bed
And I lay back in the other
Staring up through the glass ceiling
At the very real, very bland, blue Kansas sky
As she twanged and twisted
Both her legs, sparks
Flying, the odor of matches and sweat,
Me afraid to even turn my head.
Tomorrow Jon and Judy you'll read in the paper
That light, like personality, thinks.
As over a man and a woman
Lying in beds in a motel room on Kellogg St.
Without any visible means of support
There will be suspended 225 wet stainless-steel dashes
That the woman as she wakes in the late afternoon
Will explain she made to illustrate
The particular opposite of the undulatory theory of light.

ACTING SIMPLE

FOR BOB MOON

1973, THE FEMALE ARTS COMMISSIONER

She is in her nice house envisioning
Beauty spread everywhere via
Everything and she stops drinking
And eating marijuana brownies
To kick her shoes off into the Ferdinand Hodler light
That has flown from the museum where it emanates
From his painting *Day II* to Dodge City
Via the way light flies, by waves she thinks.

1988, HER MARK

Farmer Brown is pumping water out of his boots
With his new portable hand pump, reading a novel, and daydreaming
Of the days he really dreamed endlessly of girls' guts
Transforming themselves into, as he put it dreaming:
Split bald marble triangles that smelled like noxzema.
Now humming and bending to his task and reading,
He thinks the author is a man like him and thinks
"You shit-fucker, you don't write from the center of a world."

1974 AND BEYOND

Human beings, trees, mountains, and clouds
Are beginning to seem to her future husband
Like one loving circle which he represents
In his high-priced painting as a donut

Suspiciously unlike a donut. This is preparing
Him for marriage to her which will work
Because she finds his pecker incredibly ugly and hard.

1904–1906

In the mural-sized painting *Day II* by Ferdinand Hodler
"The central nude could be a priestess
Channeling the emotion of the group toward the light of day."
The legs of the five women are sure inviting
Being those kind that are tapered at the knee,
Then squarish up higher, then with a trace of thigh, just.
"Dreamlike movements and ritual gestures animate the figures."

1988

Standing that same size before the mural,
Farmer Brown and the female arts commissioner and her husband
Like it a lot and aren't able to resist stepping into it, you
Know, just stepping right into it,
And they do but they are sorry because a dream
Voice whose role in the painting is as a resource person
Says "NO FUNNY PASTRIES AND NO PUMPS HERE! HA! HA!
But my what a wonderful world you done left behind
As you pass into this painting via the little particles of light
You have become and I am putting my finger
On this last point as the world's love."

CIRCLES AND WAVES

Everyone knows the darling portions, the widening ripples,
Disappear soon and the water is there and the hard stone's sinking
And that sometimes people disappear after being beautiful or unique.

It is an immense planet, except in planes,
And then up hundreds of feet you see the lines men made but not the men.
A husband escaped to Hong Kong would be so hard to find,
Then there are those who sit listening to their phones, thinking
No number on earth can reach me now, none, none.

Myself, I am the ripple, and death's eye, so similar,
Loves me and looks into me just as long as he can.

SPEED OF LIGHT

I'm sleepy in the afternoon at the table before I can stop myself;
A phone rings across the road under a roof in a dip of a hill;
I can raise my head to see a kid grab a handful of dry sand,
Turn it over, and let it fall into the ocean.
Where I guess it drifts down thru the salt green water and disappears.
Each line, Ma Bell or GTE, has the same general tone
Unlike the omphalic telephone (hi, baby)
Or actual life, which hops among emotions
And also must admit to the scene a black locomotive with a few cars
That I'm afraid of all night.

Mongoloid star receding as red, approaching as blue
"Is in trouble" (go fast and you'll stop). If what you say is true
There's a tendency for everything to seek its human level,
That star may think too much of itself,
Blowing itself up, coming and going,
But things in the sky are so far away
That jagged hot stuff can't cut the sky's languidity
Though empty time is speeding and picking up speed
You wouldn't believe when we have a late lunch
And hysteria squats on the table like a bad dog and we let it.

Let's drive out into some other hills and have directed hallucinations
Where when we yell halloah there's an echo of an echo
And the police don't mind and the mice that if you held
To your nose smell like coffee they don't mind,
For the mind, dramatized, loses consciousness

And that's what I hate most about driving out into these hills—
Even though I swore to let things work to their full structure,
To speak my mind, to become what I beheld,
Here there is a way of forgetting your way—
Or yawn, gear, and call it a day.

Pools and yuccas must have been growing smaller
Under us, in the wet blinding air;
I listened, making the plane's engines easier to bear
Us up the aisle to pee, and my face's thick iron skin of mad fear.
It was no fade to black that made Jesus disappear
But to rise like a hedonist freaking on purity,
Thinking, "My engines are perfect, perfect—
No more lifelong state of reactions hurtling from brain to heart,
Ricocheting vice versa, yoo-hooing to each other, always
The danger of collision among the friendly beeps—"

That old doppler shift maddening in Jesus' ears no more.
We frozen in sex a few seconds, we are shady
Or forgotten as sometimes many people occupy our minds,
Many more half-formed people lie between us,
An engineless spirit passes thru, sails, and is prized
For the force with which we're paralyzed,
Yes as the sun our dear star paints a shadow
We are shady, stubby then tall, the planet top-like dizzies
And around, around, surrounds it as in a solar system cahoots or a
          drunken plan
To pickle, sculpt, or freeze a wriggly woman or man.

"Copies of Joyce, *Sporting News*, Donne, *Penthouse*, and *Time*
Would lie piled like a dagwood sandwich at his feet

As he would lie dead in dirty Manhattan that in that decade
Was itself sinking like a hammer into the sea
Or like a penis, heavy, covered with blisters and callused
Would sink in the old salty water" said I to my daughter.
See, I'd become a teacher and father, and a liar
About the future. ("What do you think doom is?"
Was the question.) Braver, I drive around it, rise,
And peer into the soup that yonder before me lies.

The moon, like a jar of gasoline washing the fingers of cars
That slowly clasped and fondled the freeway,
The winter moon (as winter's day, that gray dwarf,
Held its hands up to the power of the dark)
Bared trees of hot birds and bled richly underneath,
Copper, yellow-white manganese discharging in its pockets,
And the tears of aromatic benzine staining its jolly nose and cheeks . . .
Perhaps Santayana's mind's footsteps only tiptoe around this subject,
"The powerful solvent of American life," perhaps Crane is a big glass
        tube of words,
Moon at top, earth at bottom, pulling at the guts of women and birds.

Dear Heart, of the Skin Helmet, I report something coming
Perhaps, or coming sideways, meandering
Like the deranged Sunday drives of the Tornado Family.
Maybe. While it may be gathering we'll invoke flesh mixed with concrete;
The steps of Baltimore had an odor like your mother's knees didn't they; well
We'll use them like ack-ack, roots will be beaten into cannon,
A few Negroes singing in the trenches, the Big Radio Dangle,
Will seem like thousands, and white guys screaming in the canyon,
That'll do it or an ethnic fog we can raise wet and moaning *authenticity*
—But all I said was a great machine overhead appears to move slowly.

Notes. 1. Zebras unnoticed like heating ducts in a white room,
Exquisitely posed, poised, not frozen, ready forever . . . have forced you . . .
Notes. 1. Pneumatic stomachs, egg-assed, some teeth, hemorrhoids
To be held in awe, drawing fast, hands moving hyperactively, same
As a chimp's in any zoo, same vacuous stare
Into only that present, skinned like a tire,
Generations of artists at a twenty-three-foot rock . . .
2. Passed through Galilee a chautauqua, "The Black Crook," finale
100 women doing a clumsy ballet in cheap pink panties only,
Gone, a dozen wagons way down the road. A minute passes

And no dust. No lesson from Him upon this . . .
1. . . . have superimposed blue baboons, brown baboons, antelopes gray
        and green;
Brown rainsnakes optimistically long dangle over the frame; piles
Of shit white and brown, busy naked hunters green, brown, blue,
And white, are among countermotion of herds,
Elands and quaggas of these stains . . .
Forced to search for corridors in time, bandages
For fear's electric scratches, you see the panties Jesus saw, brown
        antelopes ravaged
In an art so volatile you can hear them choke
From your own deep steel tunnel, where the wires leak smoke.

Like things biting back and swimming on in a buried stream,
Further and further, we all argued into the night, shredding it,
One had trouble with a dream, and we decided we would change
So much we'd seem as strange and numb to those placid, supple beings
        to be born
As dear caves fondled in the minds of the wild gone
(Precious turds of warmth and safety)

Are queer to us gods of dryness and light, fluent
Ifs like a hundred fins on our hips. Well look, your breasts
Are lurid, my hysteria howls in your muscular sail,
And his living wife, as if petrified, comes back from the dead each night
    without fail.

Disappearing into a house is nothing, not scary, and if you don't stay
Years, it's OK. Disappearing down and down into some rectangles
While grinning is bitter, bitter dread
But it's framed . . . relieved by pointless chatter to your rear . . .
Why, a kiss wipes it away as if a kiss were wipers bolted
To the frame. Now the long beautiful light
Rambles into the territory of the night and people hum
In cars, arrive, slide glass doors and laugh happily.
I do that. Do you remember the powerful days
Around us like a neon fence, or squinting and crying from the brightness
    of that hope?

So what everything's falling it's only natural and it'll stop
Turn around or just stop and I'd imagine everything'd float, big turning tops
That now are massive bodies that are in the way of bodies leaves feathers
Iron and I'm afraid space is bent the nearer and nearer
To the surface the more it bends not human beings
But flecks shot inches from the planet so what
It doesn't make you turgid, dizzy, or more handsome
Let me into your arms I want to come
In the morning could we sort things out, coldly,
In the bright? Imitate the great healers of that fragmented breathless century?

The black locomotive has a schedule too
Hauling an apocalypse machine away from me and you
The sun was sweat, now it's shade as we're hidden from it

And I have moved about the house quite a bit
So these were not dreams, not versions of what seems
Nor what happens when space or love is bent
Was it before today I was molten, hopeless and mean
The ocean, which we've ignored, is receiving the sun
Thrusting, blushing and throwing up white spittle
It heaves and calls my name a little

THE VEIN

LATER

Daylight wasn't holding on, it had no more will across the river,
fingers of light were turning over like hands into the black shade,
but incandescents around houses and piers
popped and sighed, searing the gray flesh of the air,
and in this way in my imagination wounds
were being burnt closed.

Almost, there's silence. You swear there's a country
where all rivers cut deeper each year,
toss up dark, squirming life, and subside.
You swear it, and you almost remember it.

I have emptied my mind,
just as *you* ache to do
as houses stick up like sores or despair
in the heavy air
in this the light of day not holding on
as if you were shutting your eyes very slowly.

Someone brought back from a few minutes of death
should be here to tell me how calm and good death is.
Would he fear the extraordinarily powerful spotlight and the woman
walking in it a hundred yards across the river?

.   .   .

Later in your house in an atlas I'm tapping on that country
where rivers are boring deeper each year,

floods like pregnancies in rich families
spread a happy stain wider and wider,
and then the heavy green water for months
slides through those gorges, those bigger and bigger gorges.

Our country is like a piece of broken pottery
there on the page, pink and jagged.

The grass we could see five minutes ago,
and the silver, obese river,
and old memories soaking the egg of the dark,
must be edges of our imagination,
piers we dive from.

Move your finger and hold it still—
that is the sea, swimming in it
you hope for a few miles, then lose your breath.

A NOTE ON THE AUTHOR

ARTHUR VOGELSANG was born in Baltimore and educated at
the University of Maryland, Johns Hopkins University, and the
University of Iowa. He has worked for the Kansas Arts Commission
and the Pennsylvania Council on the Arts. An editor of *The
American Poetry Review* since 1974, he continues in that capacity
from his home in Los Angeles.